Moments of Time in the Light of Eternity

Mary Thomas

Faithbuilders Publishing
12 Dukes Court, Bognor Road,
Chichester, PO19 8FX, United Kingdom
www.faithbuilderspublishing.co.uk

ISBN: 978-1-913181-84-0

British Library Cataloguing in Publication Data. A catalogue record for this book is available from the British Library

All photos are from Mary Thomas and Pixabay

Formatted by Faithbuilders Publishing
Cover by Esther Kotecha, EKDesign
Printed in the United Kingdom

TABLE OF CONTENTS

CONTENTS

INTRODUCTION

For quite a few years God has been sharing His heart and encouraging me at specific moments of time especially when I was struggling with life. Over the years and as I journaled these thoughts, I began to realise that they were not just for me, but for you too, it is by no accident that you have picked up this book.

When God gave me a title for the writings, it felt like another step, a further confirmation that they were not just for me. I knew there must be a way of sharing the truths as God planted them into my heart. It would still be some years before I felt the challenge to send them to a publisher.

There is no correct way of reading this book. Each devotion stands on its own. The book can be dipped into or read from the beginning. Most contain scriptures, and a prayer. Photos accompany the writings; some have been captured at the moments of time in which I was receiving the encouragement and insight from God.

The writings are based on the verse of scripture on the next page, a challenging one that encourages us to see that nothing we experience is wasted, even when we go through hardships, pain and suffering. It is all part of our journey through life, our Christian walk, each step bringing us closer to seeing Him face to face.

What a wonderful thought!

I trust and pray that you will be inspired to catch hold of the truth that, on that glorious day all our experiences of life will be as a moment in time, the blink of an eye, as we are caught up into an eternity that will go on forever and ever. We will at last be totally fulfilled, free and complete in Him. We will be home.

Walk with me through the devotions that I believe come straight from the heart of our heavenly Father. Hear Him whisper His love and truths into your heart. Allow Him to soothe away pain and weariness; He is just a breath away.

Be blessed my fellow pilgrims, as the scripture says, don't lose heart. Keep on walking, fixing your eyes on what is yet to come.

Therefore, we do not lose heart. Though outwardly we are wasting away, yet inwardly we are being renewed day by day. For our light and momentary troubles are achieving for us an eternal glory that far outweighs them all. So, we fix our eyes not on what is seen but what is unseen, for what is seen is temporary but what is unseen is eternal.
(2 Corinthians 4:16-18)

Peace

'Peace I leave with you, my peace I give you. I do not give to you as the world gives. Do not let your hearts be troubled and do not be afraid.' (John 14:27)

I struggle with anxiety – worry – the 'what if's' of life.

Do you relate to this?

I can 'fret' over some anxious thought for a long time before I remember to talk to the Prince of Peace.

Recently, on holiday, I woke early, anxious and worrying – I had let one of those thoughts in and it had become a mountain – a storm in my mind. I had forgotten that God says, *'Do not worry'*.

I tossed and turned, stomach in knots, and then considered talking to the One who holds all my days in the palm of His hand.

'Lord', I said, *'Please give me Your peace, I am anxious, and I know You can give me Your peace that is beyond understanding'*.

And then I worried some more!

It wasn't until a few hours later, as I stood on the sea jetty, surrounded by water on both sides that I heard the voice of God, not audibly, but through His creation, pacifying me, calming my spirit, and at last giving me the peace I craved.

It was a windy morning, bright sunshine, casting wonderful shadows on the choppy sea. The water was swirling, being blown in all directions, and then I saw it – a circle of complete stillness in the water – a large area of complete calm amid the turbulent sea. I heard God speak to my heart. He said, *'My daughter, that's what I want for you – complete peace in the midst of the storm.'*

A snapshot of truth – a moment in time where everything came into perspective – God had spoken.

I would need to draw on this later in the day and the days to come. He knew where I was, and what was coming – and He knew exactly what I needed to see and hear to make His word come alive to me.

Do you need to know His peace that is beyond understanding?

Remember, He doesn't promise to take away the trouble, but He does promise His peace. Peace is not the absence of problems, but the presence of a Person, and that person is Jesus.

Before your anxious mind runs away with you, talk to the One who knows, the One who calmed the storm – He delights to give us His peace – yes, even in the midst of our storms.

"Father, thank you that perfect peace is found in You. Please help me to draw close and receive this peace to calm the storms that often rage within me. Thank you that You are always with me, you've promised never to leave. You are closer than the very breath that I breathe. I thank and praise You. Amen."

OUR DAILY BREAD

Then Jesus declared, 'I am the bread of life, whoever comes to me will never go hungry, and whoever believes in me will never be thirsty' (John 6:35)

Sitting on the beach one day, I was watching a group of seagulls gathering, waiting for the next catch of fish.

It was then that I noticed one persistent seagull squawking at another, seemingly the same size, but obviously trying to get the other one's attention. The noise was insistent, the seagull was not going to let up.

I realised – this must be a baby, a young seagull waiting to be fed by mum. Occasionally mum would fly off, only to return later with food to feed her baby.

And the squawking would begin all over again. The young seagull was obviously very hungry and totally dependent on its mum for its food.

As I sat there in those beautiful surroundings, watching, I knew a lesson, a truth was on its way. My heavenly Father was with me and was keen to show me that this was how He wanted all His children to be – hungry and dependant on Him for their food – their spiritual food.

I was reminded of a day last year, in a very different place, on a crisp cold bright winter's morning sitting in my car in a local park, early for church and needing to hear a word from God.

Glancing in my wing mirror I had spotted black crows flocking down to pick up scraps of food left over from other visitors to the park.

'That's not what I want for you', the familiar voice had said to my spirit.

'I have the choicest of foods, a feast for you to eat, I don't want you eating the scraps, or leftovers'.

I knew my Father was speaking to me.

We are so quick to grab a slice of His word and run off into our day, taking nibbles of it as we go. God wants us to feast on His word, to revel in its riches, there is so much more for us, the choicest of foods.

We need to be like that baby seagull, desperate to be fed by Him who holds such riches in His word.

There is a feast awaiting us – even today, so let's come, hungry for more, so we can be filled to then go out ourselves to feed a hungry and awaiting world.

"Lord, please help us to crave spiritual food from You. All we need is found in You and You so eagerly and generously want

to give to us. Forgive us when we pick at scraps, and don't feast on You, help us to remember that all we need You provide."

HOPE FOR THE WEARY

Those who hope in the Lord will renew their strength. They will soar on wings like eagles; they will run and not grow weary, they will walk and not be faint (Isaiah 40:31)

As I finished my run yesterday, it was early evening, a beautiful end to the day, I was alone in the field and I stood cooling off, catching my breath. I wanted to capture this quiet moment of time. I felt sad, sad for the situations in my life where I had no answers, a hurting and needy world that didn't know the answer lay in the hands of their Maker.

A heart cry went out to the One who knows and to whom nothing is impossible.

'Oh God, I feel so heavy laden, I feel I carry burdens that are not mine to carry, but I hurt for those who are so lost and without hope.'

As I stood still in the presence of my King, I knew He was there, a breath away, and I knew that He heard my heart cry. No answer came, but His presence was enough for now.

In the stillness, swallows swooped down low to the ground, skimming the grass before flying off only to turn around and skim the ground again. I watched them, they came close, and I thought how wonderful it must be to fly as they did.

Then my eyes were diverted upwards, high into the blue sky and way above me was an eagle, whose wingspan was wide and outstretched. I marvelled at how high the eagle flew, this magnificent bird was being carried along by the wind current, barely flapping its wings, as it swooped down and up again.

As I watched, I heard the familiar voice I had come to know as my Father. I knew instantly the wisdom that was to follow.

'That's how I want you to be, my daughter, high above, carried along by my Spirit. Not heavy laden, walking low and burdened, but soaring above, revived and refreshed by my Holy Spirit.'

I knew this was my Father, seeing my heavy heart and, as always, caring and wanting His best for me. He saw how hurt I felt, how helpless, but He knew that if only I would soar with Him, I could look down and see things from His perspective, then my strength would be renewed.

I had no answer for the ones who hurt, who I carried in my heart, but He had, and it was His problem, not mine, it never was.

'Father, help me to give to you those I worry about, whose lives are helpless and lost, knowing You are their answer, You know, and You are more than able to work out Your plans and purposes for their lives, if only I would let them go, releasing them to You and trusting that truly, nothing is impossible for You.'

I walked back to my car, lighter and wanting to be like that eagle, so I could go back out into the world and make a difference, knowing I serve the King who delights to work in impossible situations and who alone has the power to change lives.

LIVING WATER

'Whoever drinks the water I give them will never thirst. Indeed, the water I give them will become in them a spring of water welling up to eternal life' (John 4:14)

One day a manatee visited the canal behind our holiday villa.

Manatee or sea cows, often seen in the Gulf of Mexico, range in size from 2-4 metres and can weigh up to 590kg. They spend most of their time sleeping submerged, surfacing for air at intervals of about 20 minutes. The remainder of their time is spent grazing in shallow water. They can live in sea or fresh water and, although they can drink salt water, their main source of fluid is fresh water. They can go for extended periods of time without water but eventually must search out fresh water sources for hydration.

We were very privileged to have this visitor swim near our villa. Knowing their need and love of fresh water we turned on the hose and aimed the flow into the canal.

Before we knew it, the manatee had swum over and was opening his mouth to drink deeply. It was an amazing sight, he was an enormous creature, yet gentle and safe. We took loads of photos and videos, it's not every day you see one of these great creations of God so close.

Later that day as I reflected on our visitor, thankful to God for letting us have that experience, I knew there was a lesson to be learnt, a gem my Father wanted to share from the manatee.

Not having constant access to fresh water, manatees are known to hang around fishing docks as the catch of the day is cut up and hoses are used to wash away the remains of the fish.

We, however, have a heavenly constant supply of fresh water, a flow that never wanes or stops, is always there for us, and we don't need to go to a certain place or indeed be dependent on any man to supply that flow.

How many times do we forget that constant supply is there for us? How often do we try to satisfy our thirst through worldly supplies?

There is a river flowing for those who know the Father, it is there for anyone, if they would but come to the Giver of Life.

The manatee stayed with us for a while, mouth wide open lapping up as much water as he could, and then he disappeared under the water and was on his way.

Let us learn from his example, with hearts open wide to receive our Father's living water to fill our souls, reviving and refreshing us.

Let's drink deeply, our Father has all we need, His supply will satisfy all our needs.

"Forgive us Father when we drink from resources that are not from You. Help us to draw from Your well that never runs dry. Amen."

DARK DAYS

God is light; in Him there is no darkness at all (1 John 1:5)

One dark February morning, after heavy snowfall, I sat on a plane ready for take-off. Buckled up, I gazed out of the small window, it had been an uncertainty as to whether we would ever get away because of the weather, but here we were.

Do you struggle with winter? I often feel down, I'm not good with the dark days, the heavy skies, and the lack of sunlight.

As we took off, I was aware of turbulence, and quickly asked God for safety as the plane was buffeted by the wind.

Suddenly, we broke through the dark skies into a glorious blue – we had risen above the clouds into a wonderful sunny day – the sun streaming in through the window, the earlier dreariness gone. I could see the clouds below, but we had flown way above them.

Wow, my mood lifted, my spirit soared. I could feel the warmth of the sunlight as it rested on me and as I sat there, I heard God whisper to me.

'My light is always here my child, but sometimes it is obscured by your troubles and pain.'

Oh, what a lesson, what an insight, a wonderful visual aid. *'Thank you Lord'*, I whispered. I would remember this for a long time.

Often when we go through difficulties and hardship, the world can seem so dark. Ask God to show you a glimpse of Himself, let His light shine through and warm your spirit, and lift your heavy heart.

Remember, above all that darkness is a brilliant light, and one day we will live in the glorious light of Jesus forever – no more struggling, sorrow or pain.

But for now, don't forget, He is in our midst, surrounded by His glorious light, always here for you. Allow His love and light to filter through the darkness and touch you once more.

"Father, sometimes this life feels so dark, but thank you, You are in the midst of the darkness and Your light shines to brighten my day. Help me to see You, when I feel surrounded by difficulty and can't find my way through. Amen."

God Showing Off

The heavens declare the glory of God;
the skies proclaim the work of His hands.
Day after day they pour forth speech;
Night after night they display knowledge. (Psalm 19:1-2)

The water was crystal clear, a turquoise blue; as the wind caught the top of the gentle waves, the sea sparkled in the sunlight. The sun was climbing high in the sky, accompanied by the heat of the day, and I stood in awe of the beauty of my surroundings.

I was so thankful to be back in my favourite place, enjoying the atmosphere, soaking in the sights, sounds and smells. It was all so familiar to me. I knew our time out here was short, and I wanted to capture every moment, something to remember in the dark winter days we were facing when we arrived back home.

We have been visiting Florida for many years, and I never grow tired of the vibrancy of colour displayed through every season.

Here in the UK, we do have beautiful colours in autumn, spring and summer. But winter for me seems to dull the colours to greys and browns, and days are short of light. I wait patiently for the first signs of spring flowers, and longer hours of sunlight again.

We spent most of the day on the beach, watching the world go by, swimming and sunbathing, my husband walking the beach with fishing rod in hand scanning the shallows for a sight of fish. We were treated to a dolphin display, and a manatee swam by. I captured all these sights on camera to reflect on in the coming days.

Early evening, after cooling off at our holiday villa, we returned to the beach to watch the sun go down.

God was really showing off tonight! He created the most marvellous sunset I have ever seen. People gather on the beach every evening to watch the sun going down, and tonight God had excelled Himself. What a show He was putting on for us.

The beauty of His creation shone out; this time the sea was sparkling red and purple as the last rays of sunlight caught the tips of the gentle waves. Watching the fiery red ball of sun disappearing, God continued His light show, and I stood in awe at the effect of the colours as they danced on the surface of the water.

The Holy Spirit dropped a thought into my mind.

I believe the Lord does this just for you and me, creating these beautiful scenes to capture our attention and show off His glory, because of His great love for us and His desire for us to know Him.

I wonder have you ever stopped and wondered about the world we live in?

There was a time when I never gave it a thought, but once I came to know Him, I saw the world through different eyes. I saw beauty and majesty in creation and now I rejoice at every sunset He displays.

I watched the sun disappearing below the horizon. I had a lump in my throat, I felt so emotional with the reality of the love of my Father, as He displayed His beauty to me. I felt His smile, it was as if He was standing next to me in the coolness of the sand, just Him and me, watching His wonderful creation. I whispered a thank you to Him for allowing me to see a glimpse of His glory and as I did so I believe He had a twinkle in His eye.

When you can, take a moment to step out of your busyness, and look and ponder on all the beauty that surrounds us in this world. It's all for us, created for our pleasure, to point us to our Creator, so we can experience His love and marvel at His beauty.

Our heavenly Father loves to show off, He wants to catch our attention, so don't let's miss His moments. They are priceless.

"Father, I love Your creation, this world is beautiful, and I know You have created it all for our pleasure and to reveal Your glory. Thank you for this world You have made, help me to see You and recognise Your handiwork. Amen."

When God Seems Far Away

'And surely, I am with you always, to the very end of the age' (Matthew 28:20)

Do you sometimes feel like God is not there?

You are praying to a brick wall?

You know by faith that He is present because His word says, 'I am with you always' (Matthew 28:20)

But you choose to believe by faith because it is not your experience. You just don't feel Him near you.

I was thinking that one day, as I attempted to pray to the brick wall. Believing by faith that God could hear me, but not knowing His presence.

As always God could hear my thoughts, knew my words before they came from my mouth. I told Him I couldn't feel His presence and hadn't done so for many weeks.

As sat there, I was tempted to just get on with my day, giving up seemed easier than sitting in silence.

Then I felt Him respond to my moaning.... I didn't feel His presence, but I knew He was talking to me, encouraging me to listen.

'*I am always with you,*' I felt Him say, '*but sometimes you are too busy to notice my presence. I am in the touch of the sun upon your face. I am in the wind blowing your hair, I am in your friends smile, their kindness to you. I am in the birdsong, the flowers, the first sense of Spring in the air. I love to show you my creation, the rainbows, the sunsets, the sunrise. The movement of wind in the trees, there I am. Listen, watch, experience my touch in all these things, they are signs of my presence, all around you every day. They are signs of my love for you, my eye is always upon you looking for ways to bless you, ways to show you my love.*'

As I sat there, I realised that I do know God's presence, it's not always a feeling, but He is all around, I just get too distracted, and caught up with worldly ways.

Today I will go out expecting to see Him, feel Him, experience His closeness all around.

Why don't you try to see Him in unexpected ways? Maybe take a walk and feel the wind upon your face, that shaft of sunlight through the trees, that's Him. That bird singing as you pass, that may be Him. Look around at the wonderful creation He made just for your pleasure. Let Him warm your heart with all the wonders of His world. You may not 'feel' anything, but whoever said faith was about 'feeling'?

Knowing, really knowing, God is deeper, much deeper than that.

"Lord, help us to know, really know You, even when we don't feel You, You are always present, all around us. Help us to see You in the normal everyday things in life, and to keep talking to You, because You hear every heart cry. Amen."

Just Before the Dawn

There will be no more night. They will not need the light of a lamp, or the light of the sun, for the Lord God will give them light. (Revelation 22:5)

I woke early this morning, it was still dark, and whatever I did I just couldn't get back to sleep. Normally I would fret about this, worry that I would be tired all day, but this time, instead of fretting I tried praying and listening to the silence that is there just before the world wakes.

All of a sudden, the dawn chorus started, just one bird song and then another until it seemed like a multitude of birds were singing their hearts out. One bird sung louder than the rest, singing a variety of songs each tune different from the one before. I lay there thinking, it is still dark, why does that bird sing in the dark?

Then I heard the familiar still small voice of my Father gently speaking to me in the quietness of my mind.

I felt Him say to me, '*The bird sings because it knows that the dawn is coming*'.

What a profound thought: even though it is still dark, the bird knows and is confident that the daylight will come, the dawn is just around the corner. Because of that assurance it can sing its heart out.

In a moment of time, I knew this was another lesson for me. It is dark sometimes in my life, and I don't see the way forward, and I really don't feel like singing or worshiping God. But if I really understand, just like the bird, that the dawn is nearly here, then surely, I can sing, really sing my heart out, because the darkness will flee and the light will come.

The dawn may signify many things for us. Healing of the mind, heart, body or spirit, a lost son or daughter returning home, a relationship being restored, financial breakthrough, depression lifting.

The real and most important dawn for the believer is the final dawn of the New Day when we will eventually step into the realms of heaven and see the darkness flee for ever. In heaven, there is no day or night, for the light of our King will be all we need.

Do you long for that day? I do, but I also realise that we live in the here and now until that day, so maybe we need to be like the birds. Sing in the darkness, in the hard times, with a knowing that our own dawn will come, because our Father is faithful and will make our way clear before us.

Next time you hear the dawn chorus, remember the day is coming, the light will be here shortly, the sun will rise, and each day His grace is sufficient. Try singing out, worship our God with all your heart, if the birds can do it, then maybe so can we.

Rejoice in the Lord always. I say it again: Rejoice! (Philippians 4:4)

"Father, help us to sing to You, You are so worthy of our praise. Even in dark times You are still worthy. How You love to hear our voices. Help us to remember that a time is coming when we will rejoice with all of heaven as the final day dawns. Amen."

Revel in His Presence

'My beloved spoke and said to me, Arise, come my darling, my beautiful one, come with me' (Song of Songs 2:10)

Lying under the shade of a palm tree in my favourite place, I was relishing the cool breeze washing over me and listening to the rustling of leaves from above. I felt completely content.

All at once, the wind picked up blowing a palm branch open at an angle that allowed the heat and light of the sun to blaze down. The coolness was at once replaced by the suddenness of heat and brightness radiating down on me.

The thought came to me at once. The warmth, even the heat, of God's love and the bright radiance of His presence are quite overpowering and how little we experience these wonderful qualities of our heavenly Father?

Life is so often clouded in the shade of troubles and difficulties that get in the way of knowing His closeness, yet He is always there, always desiring for us to experience the warmth of His presence.

What are the things that shield us from Him, stop us experiencing more of Him? Maybe we are afraid of God getting too close to us?

I was lying in the shade to protect myself from the sun for safety from its harmful rays. But we as His children should never try and protect ourselves from Gods touch upon our lives, for unlike the sun's dangerous rays, our heavenly Father only has good in store for us.
In revelling in His presence, we will only receive that which is beneficial for us. More of His love, His peace, His joy. These are all gifts given to us through His grace.

As His children, He desires to lavish so much more of Himself on us.

So, let's not hide in the shade. Let's be willing to open ourselves up to Him and all He has for us. Let His brilliance shine upon and through us, for not only will we be blessed, but we will reflect something of His glory to those around us.

"Father, forgive me when I hide from You, when You are welcoming me into Your presence. It is a safe and life transforming place to rest. Help me to trust You more and run to be with You. Amen."

THE RIPPLING EFFECT

'And if anyone gives even a cup of water to one of these little ones who is my disciple, truly I tell you, that person will certainly not lose his reward' (Matthew 10:42)

My husband loves to fish. We often walk the rivers, and he will take time to watch the surface of the water to see if there is any life below.

As I sit here today at our holiday villa watching the water, it is still and calm. I talk to God about the quiet and peace and thank Him for the beauty of His creation.

Across the canal are signs of life just below the surface, small splashes disturbing the calm. Then a small fish jumps up out of the water and back down again, causing a rippling effect that spreads quickly over a large surface of the water, lasting for quite a few moments.

A small fish jumping out had a large impact for quite a time – something so small, yet causing such an effect.

It was then that I was reminded of something Jesus said in the Bible.

Jesus said that He sees a cup of water given in His name; a small act of kindness is recognised and acknowledged by our Lord.

A small act of kindness can have a rippling effect on someone's life, a smile can change their day, an encouraging word, an offer to help or pray for them, a truth shared, all these can have a rippling effect that spreads out from one small 'cup of water'.

I thanked the Lord that He quietly reminded me of this as I watched the water eventually settle down again, determined to 'give a cup of water' to someone in His name, to cause that rippling effect in another's life.

I was grateful for another valuable lesson learnt through His wonderful creation.

"Thank you, Father for teaching me how to please you, and love others with the smallest act of kindness. Help me to reach out and express your love to someone today."

FOOTPRINTS IN THE SAND

How beautiful on the mountains are the feet of those who bring good news (Isaiah 52:7)

Walking early one morning along the edge of the beach near the water's edge, the sun was just rising, shedding a beautiful light on the dawning day. I noticed an elderly man was taking his morning stroll assisted by a younger man. As they walked by me, I noticed he wore large trainers, and I found myself wondering how old he was and what his life story would be if I were to ask. His trainers left a trail of footprints, making deep imprints in the soft damp sand.

It was then that I noticed all the other footprints leaving trails of imprints, different shapes and sizes, some bare feet, some trainer footprints. Every footprint belonged to a life, well known to their Creator and some who would know their Creator as Father God.

Every trail of footprints belonged to someone travelling on the journey of life, all with different life stories to tell.

As I continued to walk, I was struck by the realisation of the value of every life, everyone a unique individual loved by God. Sadly, some footprints would belong to those who would be unaware that they were not only dearly loved by God, but also had need of a Saviour who had given His life for them.

Every person we meet is heading into eternity and God may want us to be part of helping them on the right path into everlasting life with Him. A lost eternity without God is a frightening place to live forever.

Eternity is real and relevant to every person who has lived or ever will live, and what decisions we make in this life will decide where we spend eternity. Those of us who know our Lord and Saviour Jesus Christ have no fear of death. We know where we are heading.

Do you have the assurance of heaven? Have you surrendered your life to Jesus who died for you? He longs to welcome you into His family.

As I continued walking, there were so many trails of footsteps. Each life precious to God.

Let's make sure our footprints are making a difference whilst there is time.

Let us be encouraged to look for opportunities to share the truth of our Saviour who loves us and died so we might live with Him forever.

"Father, give us eyes to see who You may put across our paths, someone who may be in need of a Saviour. Please help us not to miss any opportunity You give us to share You with others. Amen."

The Narrow Path

Walking along the beach early one morning, I noticed the straight and narrow tyre tracks of a vehicle, probably the local sheriff checking out the area. I noticed how the tracks headed towards the horizon and, interestingly, into the light of the rising sun reflected on the water. I knew I had to capture this in a photo as it reminded me of the narrow path that Jesus told us we would follow as His disciples.

I once walked the wide path. It is anything but straight. It is crooked and windy and is deceptive in its ways. I thought it was an exciting way to live, taking risks that were damaging me, but so difficult to refuse. I chose to rebel against the right way, and for a long time this felt good, my friends walked this path, and I wanted to be accepted as part of their crowd.

Years later, I would find that the path was indeed crooked in its ways. My life was messed up, I had taken so many turns and twists down wrong ways, I couldn't find the way out. Just like a maze, I turned this way and that, only to find myself in a darker place, up against a dead end.

I needed help to get off this path, but each attempt proved to be another crooked way, never leading me into light and freedom.

Then Jesus met me. He walked into my life and shone His light into my darkness, forgiving me for living life my way, guiding me onto His straight path, and into the light and love of His presence.

Sometimes the narrow path is hard and, if you are like me, you may find yourself tempted to step to the right or left, thinking the wider path may be easier to walk on for a while. In His faithfulness, our Father assures us that if we turn to the right or left, we will hear a voice behind us telling us,

'This is the way, walk in it'. (Isaiah 30:21)

In His great care and love for us, He will not let us wander too far off the narrow way, for the widened walk is deceptive and will eventually lead us down the wrong and destructive ways that will harm us. We are like sheep that can so easily be led astray. (Isaiah 53:6)

The beauty of the narrow way is that, however hard it may seem at times, every day it leads us walking onwards straight into eternity where we will see Jesus face to face. What a wonderful thought and encouraging incentive to stay on the straight and narrow path.

"Father, thank you that you lead us, encouraging us to keep to Your path. Thank you it is the safe and best way to live our lives. Please help us to listen out for Your voice, saying, 'This is the way, walk in it'. Amen."

HOME

It's that time again, when the dreaded wasps are out in force searching for a place to build their nests. The last few days, early in the morning, they have been flying into my bedroom, buzzing around, never resting as there is nowhere that is suitable indoors to build their home.

Eventually I have been able to coax them out into the open again.

Yesterday, as I did this, I felt the gentle nudge from my Father, I knew He was about to share a truth with me.

The wasps coming indoors, searching and not finding a suitable home, is a picture of our Christian life here on earth. I know I so often search out or spend time in places where I think I will find contentment and satisfaction. I may find temporary relief, but never long term, and usually very short lived.

We are not meant to find our home in anything or any place apart from the heart of God. He is our resting place, our dwelling, and only in His presence will we feel the peace and contentment that is ours in Him.

As the psalmist says,

Even the sparrow has found a home and the swallow a nest for herself, where she may have her young – a place near Your altar. (Psalm 84:3*)*

A reminder that we are made for Him, and although we live our earthly lives here on earth, our real home is in Him, in His presence, living in Him. When we search out other places to satisfy our needs, we will find they are empty and, like the wasp, they are not where we are meant to be.

How lovely is your dwelling place O Lord Almighty!
My soul yearns, even faints, for the courts of the Lord;
my heart and my flesh cry out for the living God (Psalm 84:1-2)

Is this our hearts desire? Deep down are we not desperate to experience dwelling in His place?

How much more must our heavenly Father yearn for our attention. He longs to lavish us with more of Himself. He knows this is where we will find true contentment, and one day when we step into the fullness of eternity, and see Him face to face, we will be fully complete, no more distractions, totally whole, and completely at peace.

We will truly be home!

ANGELS

One day, I was feeling low and oppressed due to an ongoing health issue. The enemy was distracting my mind from the truths of God, and I felt alone and wondered where God was, although I knew by faith He was with me as promised.

It was whilst I was walking up to the local shop that I looked up into the blue cloudless sky and was surprised to see a large thin cloud that looked like an angel, wispy and easily missed.

I felt immediately tearful and desperately wanted to believe that this was a sign, a reminder from my Father of His presence encouraging me that He knew how I was feeling.

I soon forgot about this moment of time.

A few days later, in my Bible reading I came across the verse in Hebrews 1:14

Are not all angels ministering spirits sent to serve those who will inherit salvation?

The truth is that angels play a vital part in our lives. They carry out God's will in protecting us, impacting circumstances, and sometimes delivering messages from God, as we read in the accounts of people in the Bible. Some people say they have seen an angel in physical form, but we can be sure they are around us, we who are inheriting our salvation.

Now, I know what I saw was the shape of a cloud that day, but God can use anything to speak to us and remind us He is with us.

I choose to believe that was exactly what He was doing that morning as I walked, trying to cope with how I was feeling.

One moment of time, but how easily we can miss a blessing from God, and a reminder to keep looking up, and remember we are surrounded by His heavenly army.

Colours in the Darkness

God is light, in Him there is no darkness at all (1 John 1:5)

I stood on the balcony looking out to sea.

Day was dawning over the horizon, the sun was coming up, yawning its colours, slightly hidden by low lying clouds.

I rushed for my camera, wanting to capture the array of colours from another spectacular sunrise in my favourite place. It was still quite dark, but the promise of daylight was rising, and photos of this moment were captured. I always love the way God shows off His wonderful creation just for our pleasure.

As is often the case, God was about to teach me another lesson from His beauty all around me.

As watched the show of sunrise emerging from behind the clouds, the sun's rays captured multiple colours through the gradually awakening day.

God was revealing to me that there is always colour to be found in darkness. Darkness has a way of blocking out light, causing us to see things from a different viewpoint, making life seem unbearable at times. But as sunlight starts to glimmer from behind the clouds, it often creates the most beautiful colours, even in the darkness of despair.

We may need to look with eyes that are willing to see; it's a bit like putting on sunglasses with a polaroid tint, they make colours look so much brighter. I call them my feel-good lenses. They change the way we see things, putting a different light on the world around us.

Trust Him in the shadows of life and ask Him to show you the kaleidoscope of colours to be seen in the darkness. They are there, and He will show you. Colours in darkness may appear as kindness or care shown to you, a smile from a stranger, a glimpse of eternity through an everyday moment, maybe a rise in faith to believe for the impossible. Hope for the future.

The darkness is temporary, it will pass, and one day, when this world is rolled away, a bright new morning awaits us in Jesus.

But until the dawn of that glorious day, we have His light to brighten our way. Look up, search for the colours, even when life seems so hard.

God wants to bring colour into your days. Trust Him, He will.

PANORAMIC VIEW

The Lord looked down from His sanctuary on high, from heaven He viewed the earth (Psalm 102:19)

One beautiful sunny morning, sitting on the balcony of our villa, I discovered the panoramic view on my camera! Now I am no expert at taking photos, but I love capturing moments of beauty or interest, so this was a real find for me!

I tried taking a panoramic photo from where I was sitting.

God chose this moment of time to teach me a valuable lesson.

He has a panoramic view, not only of the world, but also of our lives. He has the perfect perspective on everything we experience.

We often get locked up in the 'present' of our struggles. And life can be hard living in the present. We don't see the way forward, we can't see a way through.

Our Father though, sees the beginning and the end, not only of our struggles and difficult times, but the whole of our lives. In His word, our heavenly Father says,

All the days ordained for me were written in Your book before one of them came to be (Psalm 139:16)

He who created us, saw us before we were born, knows every moment of our lives.

We may not know how things will pan out, we may not even know how we may get through the next minute of time, especially through troubles and difficulties, but our Lord does. And He can and delights to help us through. Isn't that a comforting thought?

If we really allow ourselves to believe this is true, surely that means we can trust Him with every moment that stretches out before us.

Ask Him for His perspective. See your situation through His eyes. We may be caught up in time here, but we are headed for a timeless eternity, never-ending peace and joy that will be ours forever.

"Father, thank you that You see the whole of our lives, the bigger picture. You know our present and our future. We are safe in Your hands. Amen."

Writing in the Sky

I don't know about you, but do your ever feel as if you have let God down? You don't feel worthy of His love, or you are tempted to feel that God is not enough?

How easily we let these thoughts in, and I was struggling with these same thoughts as our holiday came to an end and we were awaiting our drive to the airport.

We'd had a lovely few weeks, but I had experienced fear and anxieties, I had let the enemy feed me lies and, even though I had asked for God's help, I had still used my own ways of dealing with anxiety, my old coping methods, to get me through.

As we walked around the lake, biding time, it was a beautiful morning. The sky was a clear blue and there was a stillness in the air, I was making the most of the beauty and warmth, knowing we were heading back into a British winter.

As we continued to walk, I was gradually aware of a distant droning sound, disturbing the peace of the day. I was irritated, and saw it as an intrusion. I looked up to find the source of the noise. High in the sky I could see a light aircraft, seemingly practising some acrobatic move. But as I watched I realised the plane was writing something.

My first reaction was to think it was a proposal. Some guy spending hundreds on hiring a plane to write a love message to his possible bride to be. As I watched, my heart started to stir, I began to recognise the first letter was a J. I soon realised that the plane was spelling out 'Jesus' in the sky. My next thought was that this was going to be a gospel message, how amazing. Over the next few minutes, much to my shock, the plane spelt out a message that was personally for me... Jesus loves U. I knew God was speaking straight to my heart, as I felt unlovable due to how I was feeling about myself. Surely, I had let God down, but here He was, spelling out His love message to me.

I looked around to see if anyone was noticing this. People around me seemed disengaged. How could they be ignoring this message in the sky?

As if this was not enough, the plane then moved positions as the words started to fade and began to spell out another few words. Shocked I read, Jesus 4gives U, just ask.

By this time there was no mistaking God was speaking to me. I was reading a personal love message from my Father, who knew how I was beating myself up, and wanted to let me know He knew my thoughts, loved me and forgave me. He would go to any extreme to show how much I was worth to Him.

On returning home to the UK, I did a search on the Internet to see if I could find who was behind this. I found a small organisation that felt called by God to write His love messages in the sky. The team would pray, seeking to find out what God wanted to say and where in Florida they were to write His messages. That day they had felt the place where I was walking was the area God wanted to write His message in the sky.

That's how much and how far our heavenly Father will go at times, to speak to us. I still find it hard to believe He would do that for me. But not only has it blessed me, but lots of other people as I have retold the story.

For the man who flies these planes, it was such an encouragement to hear feedback from a heart touched by their obedience.

Long may they fly!

Everlasting Arms

The eternal God is your refuge, and underneath are the everlasting arms. (Deuteronomy 33:27)

I was sitting on our holiday villa balcony inwardly crying out to God.

'Lord, I am struggling to focus on You, to know You are here with me. I have no real times alone with You, so much distraction, I am battling with the all too familiar anxiety, feelings of homesickness, and I feel guilty to be in such a beautiful place yet struggling with such minor issues against the bigger issues of life.'

How ungrateful I felt. Yet, I told myself it was ok, that I needed to be still and know that God was God, and to also know that He was always interested in me and everything that was worrying me, however small. I desperately needed to know that God was still in control and able to comfort me.

As I sat watching the world go by, I looked out to sea. I focussed on the Skyway Tampa Bridge that was on my horizon; it is massive and connects the island with the mainland. I could just make out the cars driving over the bridge. I had looked at this view every day of our holiday. But this day, God had something to say about it

I felt the stirring in my spirit, a sense that God was watching with me.

My heavenly Father had read my thoughts and knew I needed encouragement from Him. I felt Him whisper to my heart:

'See that bridge – how it supports the weight of all those cars? How much more am I able to carry you in my arms, my precious child?'

What a difference those few words made to me. I sat there knowing the power of knowing I was fully known, understood and important to the Creator of the whole world, who wanted to and was able to carry me in His arms.

"Thank you, Lord, that we are never insignificant to You. You are our heavenly Father, who takes great interest in every thought, feeling, every small detail of our lives. Nothing is ever too small to bring to You. May we rest in Your everlasting arms today. Amen."

WAITING WITH EAGER EXPECTATION

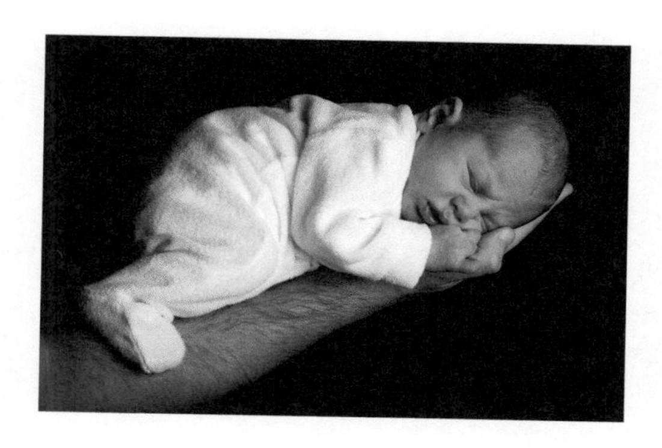

Yesterday we found ourselves waiting expectantly for news of the birth of our second grandchild. We tentatively kept the phone near to us, hardly daring to leave it unattended. We tried to focus on work much needed in the garden, but our minds were elsewhere.

What was happening? When was baby going to make an entrance? Would it be a boy or girl? Hard to imagine another baby in the family, knowing that nothing was going to stop him or her coming, but the timing was out of our hands.

Finally, the phone rang, the news came, a beautiful baby boy had entered this world. Another life to love.

In amongst the waiting a scripture had come to mind:

We know that the whole creation has been groaning as in the pains of childbirth right up to the present time. Not only so, but we ourselves, who have the first fruits of the Spirit, groan inwardly as we wait eagerly for our adoption to sonship, the redemption of our bodies. For in this hope we were saved. But hope that is seen is no hope at all. Who hopes for what they already have? But if we hope for what we do not yet have, we wait for it patiently. (Romans 8:22-25)

Are we waiting expectantly and eagerly for our future glory? Do we ponder on what is to come when this world is transformed into the new creation of the fullness of eternity?

Life has a way of distracting us. I wonder, if we were to see everything in the light of what is to come, would it make a difference in the way we live or go through difficult, sometimes tragic, seasons? When we see the monstrosities that occur in this world now, don't we sometimes long for God to say 'Enough!'?

The last words recorded by Jesus in the Bible are, *'Yes I am coming soon'* (Revelation 22:20)

Just like our waiting for the new grandchild, who was coming soon, Jesus wants us to remember so is He. We just don't know when.

We have this hope, the best is yet to come, and come it will. Every day we are walking towards heaven, step by step. In our hearts, we are already home. My prayer for you is that you will not give up your hope, you will eagerly await your redemption, especially during the dark days.

"Lord when we struggle through difficult times, when we see the injustices in this world, when we feel like it's all too much, and we want to give up, please help us to remember the hope that we have in You. A day is coming, when You will make all things new, and there will be no more suffering, or pain or tears. Thank you Jesus, Your words are faithful and true. Our hope is in You."

Eye of the Storm

Jesus calms the Storm, Matthew 8:23-27.

Then he got into the boat and his disciples followed him. Suddenly a furious storm came up on the lake, so that the waves swept over the boat. But Jesus was sleeping. The disciples went and woke him, saying, "Lord, save us! We're going to drown!"

He replied, "You of little faith, why are you so afraid?" Then he got up and rebuked the winds and the waves, and it was completely calm.

The men were amazed and asked, "What kind of man is this? Even the winds and the waves obey him!"

When life situations and our thoughts are in chaos, it can feel as if we are being swirled round and around, never settling and resting, unable to be still.

I was worrying, living with fear, and I craved to know the stillness of God. Our house move was delayed again, and news was spreading of the Coronavirus around the world.

God showed me a picture in my mind of a hurricane, I could see the force of the wind swirling around, but as I watched I found myself focussing on the eye of the storm. That completely still place in the middle of a hurricane where the wind dies down and all is still.

'This is where I want you to rest', I felt my Father whisper to me. *'This is my safe place, the place of peace where all is calm.'*

I longed to be in that place where my Father was. He was in the midst of the storm, resting, everything under His control. I remembered the story in the Bible where Jesus and His disciples were in the boat whilst a storm raged around them. Jesus was asleep! In their panic and terror, the disciples called out to Jesus asking if He didn't care that they might drown.

Do you relate to this? Are you like one of the disciples in the boat, questioning if God really cares or even knows the storm you are experiencing in your life?

In the Bible story, Jesus stood up and spoke to the storm saying, 'Be still!' And the storm died down, demonstrating His sovereignty over chaos.

Now, we may not physically be on stormy seas, but life can feel like we are. Jesus may not immediately stand up and still our storm, but He can be our safe place in the centre of the howling winds.

That's exactly where He wants us to be, unaffected by all that is around us. Totally safe in His presence, trusting that He is more than able to lead us beside still waters, to rest.

Does your heart cry out for peace? Real peace only comes with the presence of our Saviour, who promises to give us His peace that is beyond understanding. (Philippians 4:7)

Ask Him, He knows where you are, He knows exactly what is going on in your life, and He delights to draw near and still your restless heart.

"Father, draw us into Your place of peace, amid our storms. That still quiet place where Your presence is tangibly felt. You love to draw us near, help us to shelter in You even when the winds of fear and trouble are surrounding us. Thank you Lord, that You are the Master of chaos, nothing is outside of Your control. Help us to lean into You and trust You more. Amen."

Max Block

God can speak through all things, if we would only have ears to hear.

Even through a tube of suntan lotion!

Another day of struggling with the battle for the mind was occurring. It is so easy to listen to the world view when difficulties arise. It sounds true, full of authority, but it can have the power to crush us with negative thoughts that dampen the Spirit of God.

As I write, we are in the middle of a lock down due to the coronavirus, and it is difficult to see a way through. I had read the news, and felt the hopelessness of the situation. I felt the familiar sense of anxiety rising within me once again.

My eyes were averted to a tube of suntan lotion placed on the shelf and I read the words, MAX BLOCK, and immediately felt God was speaking to me, cutting through the negativity to bring His light into my darkness.

'My child, you need to protect your mind as well as your skin! I have provided the protection you need through my armour. Put it on, and stand firm in my Son. The battle is mine, you need only be still.' (Ephesians 6:10-17; Exodus 14:14)

At first, I thought it funny that God could use a tube of suntan lotion to speak. But then I was reminded that He who has the control of all the whole world, once spoke through a donkey's mouth, of all things, and will use anything to get our attention. (Numbers 22:28)

I had to play my part in putting on the full armour of God, taking captive every thought, making it obedient to Christ, (2 Corinthians 10:5) and protecting my whole being by clothing myself in Christ. God would do the rest.

Don't we all need maximum protection from the world's wisdom, and the enemy of our souls? How easy is it to allow negative thoughts to invade our minds? It's not easy to constantly be aware of how our thoughts are feeding our minds. We get distracted, and before we know it, we are on the downward spiral.

But with the Spirit's help, and by constantly feeding our minds on the truth, the word of God, we will become more discerning in recognising when wrong thoughts are entering our minds.

Remember. MAX BLOCK. All over God protection. Then we can be strong in the Lord and in His mighty power. (Ephesians 6:10)

"Father, forgive me when I allow fear, anxiety and negative thoughts to invade my mind. Please help me to remember the protection I have in You and to put on Your armour, standing firm in You. All the protection I need is found in You. Thank you Lord, Amen."

Worship

Do you need healing?

Maybe you have a physical ailment, or maybe it's emotional healing from past or present hurts you are asking God for – sometimes crying out for?

I had been asking God for over two years for physical healing from nerve damage in my mouth. This particular morning it was bad – the pain was really getting me down. I was finding it hard to focus on anything, I felt anxious and low, and the fact that God seemingly was not answering my plea for healing was difficult to understand.

I knew He was my heavenly Father to whom all power belonged. I knew He could heal – one word from His mouth, that's all it took. This is the God who created the world by His powerful word.

So, I pleaded again, also asking for wisdom to know if there was anything more I could do, was I missing something? Was there another specialist, another drug? I needed help now!!

And then my answer came, I clearly heard Him say to me, '*Worship Me*'.

What! This was my answer? God was asking me to worship Him – this was my way forward? Two words I did not want to hear. But, deep in my spirit I knew. I knew this was God's 'now' word for me. His answer to my heart's cry.

So, I told Him I would, and I did, all the way into work.

And I have worshipped and worshipped even though no physical healing has come about. But I have come to know deep down, my worship through pain is very special to Him.

My mouth is still not healed, and now, years later, I feel at peace about it. My heavenly Father knows – He knows what I need and what is best for me, and somewhere in the darkest place, to worship Him is more powerful than any physical healing – the sacrifice of praise so pleases our King.

And, I know one day, if not in this life then in eternity, I will be healed. Totally, completely – so for now I will keep on worshiping Him.

Why don't you try singing a song to Him, even in your pain, whatever that may be? Feel His smile, experience His comfort, and know the power of His presence as you bring a sacrifice of praise to Him. He is so worthy of our worship.

Through Jesus, therefore, let us continually offer to God a sacrifice of praise – the fruit of lips that openly profess his name (Hebrews 13:15)

Prayer

Do we really believe that God hears our prayers?

It's challenging to keep going in prayer when we don't see the answers or feel Him near.

But it's thrilling and so rewarding when we see an answer to prayer within hours or even minutes of asking.

After a run one day I was sitting, cooling off in my car, listening to a worship song about how our prayers are compared to sweet-smelling incense to God.

What an extraordinary thought! As I was dwelling on this, I noticed opposite in a field was a huge pile of manure. What a comparison, the smell of that manure and our prayers to God.

We often think of our prayers as a feeble effort, dare I say even like that pile of manure!

We may struggle to make the effort to talk to God and then when we do, we feel our prayers are just rubbish.

But our God sees them as a fragrant offering to Him. Even those shed through tears and heart cries. How our Lord loves our prayers. Each one precious and collected by Him, not one of them is lost.

Prayer is key to our intimacy with Him. It's as if we were talking to a close friend pouring out our desires, needs and thanks.

Don't ever give up talking to God. And don't ever be robbed of talking to your Father by believing the lie that your prayers are not good enough, or effective, or even the right ones to pray.

Your heavenly Father loves hearing your voice, and sees the heart behind your prayers, so keep persevering even when it feels hard and you want to give up.

I truly believe when we finally arrive home, we will get a glimpse of the bigger picture, why some prayers took longer, how God was busy at work answering, working out His plans and answers to our heart cries.

Keep going, keep praying, He hears, He answers. He is a faithful Father.

Let my prayer be as like the evening sacrifice, that burns like fragrant incense rising as my offering to You as I lift my hands in surrendered worship (Psalm 141:2 The Passion Translation)

Power of His Spirit.

The day was bright and sunny, the water glistening, catching the sun's rays. It was a beautiful scene and I settled down in my chair to watch the world go by.

As I sat there on the beach watching the boats sail by, I noticed one boat that didn't seem to be going anywhere. It was a windy day, and the incoming tide was causing the sea to move fast in many different directions. This particular boat had the sails up but was being buffeted by the strong wind, at times going around in circles, at other times drifting aimlessly.

I watched the other sailing boats, some with sails up, some with their sails down, but they were all charting a course through the choppy sea, heading out of the channel into the open waters, seemingly with no difficulty.

I was wondering what was wrong with the boat. Then I realised, these other boats had their motors running. They were powered up and therefore had no problems cutting through the water.

As I sat there watching, I felt the Spirit within me use this as a visionary aid to remind me about the power of the Holy Spirit within all those who love and serve the Lord.

We have His Holy Spirit always with us to guide us and strengthen us enabling us to live this life with His help, keeping us on His path. We can know the truth of who God is, we can even carry on our lives believing and knowing He is with us, but if we haven't asked for the power of His Holy Spirit to fill us each day, we can end up doing things in our own strength, getting weary and heavy laden as we attempt to live this Christian life. We can be tossed around, just like that sailing boat, without direction or power, just because we have not asked for God's infilling of His Holy Spirit.

It seems such an easy thing to ask for each morning, asking God to fill us and enable us to live through the power of His Spirit, but in fact it is a very powerful request, and can make an enormous difference to our day in whatever we may face. It also reminds us of our reliance on God's help, we can't live well without His enabling and He promises to give us all we need. In fact, He is very eager to do so.

I was thankful for this reminder, and aware that I so often forget to pray for His Holy Spirit to fill me afresh each day.

I watched the sailing boat on and off for a few hours, and maybe it was intentional that the motor was not running. Maybe there was something they needed to learn through working with the sails.

As I packed up to go home the boat had disappeared from view, the tide was in, and I was leaving the beach with another teaching from my Father to think about and more importantly to put into practice.

If you then, though you are evil, know how to give good gifts to your children, how much more will your Father in heaven give the Holy Spirit to those who ask him! (Luke 11:13)

PEARL OF GREAT PRICE.

Sitting outside the beach hut, I sensed the peace of God surround me. Relaxing into the chair, I quietened down to soak up my surroundings. This was the first time I had been down to our beach hut on my own, and I was eager to rest and enjoy having nothing to do but watch the world go by. I could hear the waves crashing onto the shingle, the tide was incoming, there were not many people about as the weather was on the turn, summer was receding, and the sun had disappeared behind some clouds.

As I sat, I was aware of a beeping noise in the distance getting closer. Now and then it stopped, only to start up again, an irritating interruption to the peace of the moment. I looked around to see the source of the noise and saw a man using a metal detector, close by, skimming the shingle until the beeping noise indicated something metal underneath.

Instantly I heard the still small voice of my Father say to me, 'You are worth far more than this'. Knowing there was more to come, I waited for an understanding of what this meant. I was reminded of the parable that Jesus told, of the hidden treasure and the pearl. Jesus is firstly talking about the

Kingdom of God being like treasure; when a man found it, he sold all he had to buy the field.

But it was the second half that my mind focussed on, and I began to understand what God was encouraging me to see. He is the merchant and we are the pearl, bought at great price, nothing less than His death, that's the price of our lives to Him.

The man searching for 'treasure' with his metal detector was eager to find buried coins or other metals, but my Father was telling me that I was of much more value than this. I was the pearl, the fine pearl, a precious jewel to Him, He gave up everything to have me. And He did this for you too. This parable is often misunderstood, many believe the kingdom of God is the pearl. But it is you. You and I are the pearl. God so loved us He gave His life for us; let that truth soak into your very being. It is transforming.

As I continued to dwell on this, the metal detector man had moved on, the irritating interruption had dissipated, and I once again sensed the peace of God surround me.

I was astounded that God would lead me to come down to the beach hut, this first time on my own, to allow me to hear Him tell me how precious and valuable I was to Him. Something I needed to be reminded of so much.

By now the clouds had darkened and a light rain was in the air, the wind had picked up and I was unable to sit outside anymore. I packed away my things and decided to shut up the hut and head home; it was not until later that day I began to realise how amazing an outing it had proven to be.

'Again, the kingdom of God is like a merchant, looking for fine pearls. When he found one of great value, he went away and sold everything he had and bought it'. (Matthew 13:45-46)

The Wisdom of God

I really needed to hear from my Father as I walked around our local park. We were in the process of moving to a new house and changing area from where we had lived for over 30 years. The Coronavirus was on the horizon, and although I knew deep down this move was part of God's plan for us, I was fretting and wanted to keep phoning round to push the move forwards.

As with most house moves, there were delays and interruptions and nothing was happening to plan. I was frustrated and wanting to sort it all out, but also aware that my husband's approach was different to mine, taking it all in his stride.

I walked on my usual path, talking to my heavenly Father, desperate to hear a confirmation that all was well, some encouragement that this move really was His plan and He had it covered. I recognised my impatience and irritations with my husband being so calm with it all. I would have to take charge and chase up all those involved in the move to push things ahead if he wouldn't!

As I continued to walk, I hardly noticed anything around me. On my usual walks, I would be looking around, smiling at people passing, hearing the bird songs, being thankful for the wonders of creation. But this day I plodded on, splashing through the puddles, wading through the mud, oblivious to the scenery passing me by.

I was on my return by now, frustrated that I hadn't heard any encouragement from God, nothing! I realised I had been walking with my head down all the way but now as I looked up, seeing the carpark in the distance, I noticed a few horses in the nearby field. I had seen them before on other days but had not even acknowledged them as I walked straight by them earlier.

This time, my eyes were fixed on them, and I knew my Father was capturing my attention. I heard Him whisper lovingly in my ear, *'Do not be like the horse or the mule'*.

I knew instantly this was something from His word. I had read it lots of times and felt the power of His conviction coming on me.

As I got back to the car, I looked up the scripture on my phone.

I knew my Father was telling me to calm down, to stop trying to push ahead, to let Him take the lead, as He would guide the move, He was trustworthy. I didn't need to be like a horse or mule who don't 'have the understanding' of being led by a faithful Father.

I felt ashamed at my pushiness and lack of faith that God would see us through this transition to a new home, wasn't it His idea in the first place?

I let His unfailing love and peace surround me again, after asking forgiveness for wanting to do it my way!

I would need to remember this lesson taught me on a rainy muddy winter day, as the weeks ahead proved testing, and many times I tried to push ahead in my own strength, only ending up feeling miserable and anxious.

Now, almost a year after the move, I can look back and see His hand every step of the way. We made it into our new house three days after the first national lockdown due to Coronavirus, a miracle in itself, as the removal company closed the following day.

How often do we try to do things our way, running ahead thinking we know best, ending up frustrated by our plans again coming to nothing?

I'm sure our heavenly Father watches over us with a twinkle in His eye. Waiting patiently for us to stop rushing around and look up to Him. It's a hard lesson to learn, to rest in His unfailing love and trust that He has our lives all planned out.

I always think back to those horses in the field when I am flustered, trying to push plans to work. But I am very thankful that God spoke so clearly to me that day, thankful that His word has the power to stop us in our tracks, and that He would so lovingly show me that I need only stop, look up and put my trust back in Him.

I will instruct you and teach you in the way you should go;
I will council you with my loving eye on you.
Do not be like the horse or the mule, which have no understanding
but must be controlled by bit and bridle or they will not come to you.
Many are the woes of the wicked,
But the Lord's unfailing love surrounds the one who trusts in Him.
Rejoice in the Lord and be glad, you righteous;
Sing, all you who are upright in heart! (Psalm 32:8-11)

Snatches of Conversation

Sitting against the sea wall, below the tow path, I am watching the water. The tide is up, creating a stillness, a quietness, water lapping near my feet. This is one of the places I go to be with God.

As people walk past me above, I listen to snippets of their conversation, just small pieces of their chat. A moan about a back problem, a new coat they are wearing, problems at work, at home, a bit here and a bit there as they walk by.

The familiar voice from my Father stops me in my tracks. I sense the smile on His face as He gently tells me that this is a bit like my prayer life with Him. A bit here and a bit there.

I realise this is so true and tell Him I'm sorry for my lack of persistence in prayer. I start well and then within minutes I get distracted by a bleep from my phone, a thought passing through my mind, and before I know it, I have interrupted my time with Him.

But, as I sit here, I feel no condemnation, just a sadness and ache from Him as He knows how much more I could receive from Him if I just gave Him the time. He is patient and persists in getting my attention. Here I am surrounded by His marvellous creation, I am aware of His mercy and grace towards me. I thank Him for His forgiveness to me for not giving Him the time He deserves.

Yet, I am weary in prayer, some prayers are more than thirty years old. But, sitting here I am so aware that I am talking to the King of Kings who delights to spend time with me and has the power to change any situation with one word from His mouth.

If only I could grasp how much He desires my attention, maybe I would be more eager to linger in His presence. It's not just about the asking, it's about revelling in His presence, enjoying Him just for who He is.

As I continue to think about this, I am reminded of a time recorded in the Bible when we get a glimpse of Jesus needing to be alone and spend time with His Father.

One of those days Jesus went out to a mountainside to pray, and spent the night praying to God. (Luke 6:12)

May I crave that quality time with my Father, where I give Him undivided attention, not just giving Him snatches of conversation.

I notice the tide has turned and is now receding and the seagulls are actively swooping down to catch fish. They are noisy and once again I am distracted from my focus on God. How easily this happens.

'Father please fill me today with your Holy Spirit to help me engage with You more. I need you so much.'

It's then that I notice that it has gone quiet behind me. No longer are people passing by. The light is fading and it's time to go home. I am thankful to God for sharing His heart, the gentle challenge to spend time with Him,

If His Son Jesus needed this when He was living on earth, how much more do I?

Seeds of Hope

Do you ever feel like you are buried deep beneath hard and seemingly impossible situations? Maybe the Coronavirus pandemic closed you in, physically and mentally, with its restrictions, fear of infection and lack of social interactions; your old life buried underneath layers of rubble and heaviness.

I was taking a walk a while back. It was bitterly cold, snow was in the air, and I was wrapped up well against the biting wind. We were nearing the end of winter, and I was a looking for signs of spring, anything that would remind me of lighter days and warmer weather to come.

Then I saw it, a small clump of tiny green shoots, poking out from under a pile of dead leaves. I recognised them as daffodil shoots, reaching up from underneath to seek the light of day.

They hadn't been freshly planted, they had laid dormant during the winter months, buried deep under layers of mud and dead foliage, and now it was time to grow, their season to surface above the earth had arrived.

Hope rose within me. Seeds of hope filled my mind. It did feel like we were in the dead of winter with the 'beast from the East' weather, but a new season was coming and nothing was going to stop it. We may feel that life as we used to know it has been buried, long gone, and we can't see a way up again. There is hope, new life will come, we will rise again, to life, maybe not as we knew it, but how God fashions it to be.

A few months passed and I found myself on another walk, a walk down memory lane. I was visiting a place where I had spent many a happy holiday in a caravan park with my family. I stopped the car to walk down the lane. Spring had arrived, primroses were growing in the hedgerows, birds were singing their spring songs and, although rain fell, nothing could dampen the sense of familiarity and memories of a young and carefree childhood joy were flooding my being. I felt the tears flow as I remembered the happy holidays spent here.

I realised this child-like joy had been buried in later years as difficulties of life had overwhelmed my spirit. I prayed as I walked, grieving for the carefree years that had been stolen and forgotten. But I was thankful to my Father for reminding me that, as a child of His, I could know healing for the grief, and I asked Him if I could experience the freedom of living as a joyful child of His.

As I write today, it is Easter Sunday, one of the greatest days in history when we remember the resurrection of Jesus Christ from the dead. I'm excited at the thought of celebrating Easter Sunday later with other Christians, I thank God for the hope He desires to give us when all seems dead and meaningless.

Jesus knew the experience of burial, and in His resurrection He has provided new hope and joy to all who would believe in Him. If our Saviour rose from the grave, so can we, whatever that 'grave' may signify for us.

As His people, we look forward to that final day when our joy will be complete as we enter the fullness of eternity and see Him face to face. We will live forever in His presence.

I'M ANGRY, GOD!

Is it ok to be angry with God?

I am today!

'Lord, I know You are the One who created the heavens and the earth. You are the One who parted the red sea. You, with one trumpet blast brought down the walls of Jericho. You are the one who threw the stars into space, and yet You know the very hairs on my head. You know me intimately, you can heal with one word from Your mouth, one touch of Your cloak and the woman with the issue of blood was healed – instantly. I've seen you heal others and know it is Your will to answer the heart cry of Your children.

So, why don't You heal me? Why Lord? What is the purpose behind leaving me in pain and disability to carry out my life with the limits of a bad back?!

I could serve you so much better if I didn't do everything with pain. I can't stand for long, I can't sit for long, I can't... but you know, don't you Father?'

You know, and that's where I stop. I've been down this path of angry prayer many times over the past four years, and always ended up with just knowing that my heavenly Father knows, and its ok to be angry with Him, He can take my tantrums. He is a loving Father who is gracious enough to allow us to rant and forgive us for our anger.

God wants us to be real with Him. He sees our thoughts and inner turmoil; it is far better to let it out and expose it all to His light.

The Bible is full of His people ranting at Him, the Psalms are raw and real. I'm so glad God allows us to see that the people in His word are just like us: same emotions, same struggles, they let God down just as we do. Yet, they knew of His goodness, His faithfulness and forgiveness, they knew the new beginnings with God, sometimes daily. And so do we.

We can rant and rave all we like, as long as we don't stop there.

Let us always remember that God is good all the time. Yes, all the time. Even when everything is falling apart, His promise is: *God works for the good of those who love Him, who have been called according to His purpose*. (Romans 8:28)

I feel the calm and let His peace rise again, I've had my say, and my Father has heard. He heard even before I spoke a word. I rest in the knowledge that He can and does heal, instantly, or over a long time, and if not in this life, in the life to come.

He is our perfect Father, He knows what is best for us, and it may not be what we think it should be. Keep seeking and asking and being real with Him. Voice out your hurts and pain, He is big enough to take it, but then allow Him to hold you tightly in His loving arms, and heal the hurt, soothe the anger, speak truth over you.

Submit to His will, His wisdom, He can pick you up and move you on.

One day we will understand, but for now, trust Him with all your heart, and don't lean on your own understanding. (Proverbs 3:5)

He is enough.

The Stuck Needle

Growing up in the 60s, we listened to vinyl records that we bought in a music shop. I had a large collection, mostly pop music, and I had a record player. I can so clearly remember taking the record out of its sleeve, placing it on the turntable turning on the switch and watching the mechanics of the record player as the arm came over and lowered the needle onto the record at just the right place and then the music began.

As I reminisced on this, I remembered how occasionally the needle would get stuck. The same piece of music would play repeatedly. The only way to stop this was to manually pick up the arm, lifting the needle off the record and placing it back in its stand.

The reason for this was usually because there was a scratch on the record, some damage, creating a groove, so the needle would get stuck when it reached that place, every time.

This was so annoying, and sadly the record would be permanently damaged.

Our thinking can be like this. We so easily have thoughts that get stuck in our minds. These thoughts can go around and around, causing anxiety and sometimes fear and tension. We try to put them to the back of our minds, only to find minutes later they have returned to the forefront again.

It may be an argument we have had and we go over the words spoken, anger rising as we think of what we would like to say if we had a chance. It may be something that has occurred that has worried us, a situation at work, an illness, an accident, a fear of something coming up, and our minds go around trying to find a solution, a way through, something that will make things better. It really could be anything that causes us unrest in our mind, and we get stuck, just like the record with the scratch on it. There is a saying that goes, 'You sound like a broken record', which means to repeat something over and over in an annoying fashion. Have you experienced any of this? I know I have.

Before I was a Christian, I would use any number of coping mechanisms to blot out these tormenting thoughts – drink, pills, anything that would calm my mind, but the pesky thoughts had a way of returning into my thinking, filling my mind, causing me great anxiety, worry and often sleepless nights. I was stuck.

In later years I became a Christian, but I still struggle with mind games – thoughts that won't go away, and I can find myself churning on them until I remember I now have a Saviour who says,

'Come to me, all you who are weary and heavy laden and I will give you rest.' (Matthew 11:28)

'Peace I leave you, my peace I give you' (John 14:27)

I can now give the turmoil to Him and, just like the arm of the needle stuck on the record, He lifts the damaging thoughts off me and replaces them with His peace. He delights in doing this. The thoughts may return but each time I can reach out to Jesus and He willingly lifts them off me.

The Bible tells us in Philippians 4:6-7 'Do *not be anxious about anything, but in everything, by prayer and petition, with thanksgiving, present your requests to God. And the peace of God, which transcends all understanding, will guard your hearts and your minds in Christ Jesus.'*

These verses are followed by verse eight which encourages us to think about whatever is true, noble, right, pure, lovely and admirable.

A real antidote to worry and churning thoughts.

It's not easy though, but with practice and the Holy Spirit's help we can experience our minds being transformed by the power of God.

No more stuck records, no more tormenting thoughts churning around in our minds for hours on end.

Don't allow yourself to be like a stuck record.

Ask Jesus to help you, He will. He loves to lift us out of turmoil and usher in His peace.

What a truly wonderful Saviour we have.

"Father, please help us to surrender our anxious thoughts to You. Thank you, you promise to give us rest and an easy burden. Help us not to get stuck in the 'what ifs' and worries of life. Thank you Lord, Amen."

Elijah was a Human Being Just like Us

The Bible says that Elijah was a human being just like us (James 5:17). What a statement!

You can read about this great man of God in 1 Kings chapters 17-20 in the Bible. A man who had extraordinary encounters with God. A man who raised back to life the son of a widow at Zerepath after he had died. At Mount Carmel Elijah challenged the 450 prophets of Baal, proving that the Lord is the one true God.

We see a man who prayed earnestly that it wouldn't rain for three years, and it didn't, until he prayed again for the drought to end and then the rain came.

We read of miracle after miracle taking place and marvel at his faith, and the way God displayed His glory through him.

And then, Jezebel comes onto the scene, the evil wife of King Ahab. After hearing from her husband all that had taken place and the slaughtering of 450 prophets of Baal, Jezebel sends a messenger to say to Elijah,

'May the gods deal with me, be it ever so severely, if by this time tomorrow, I do not make your life like one of them.' (1 Kings 19:2)

In a moment of time, this mighty man of God became afraid, he made the shift from victory to fear, and he ran for his life – terrified!

We may ask, 'How could this happen?'

After seeing and experiencing the power of God in ways we can only imagine, he believed Jezebel was going to kill him. Jezebel became very powerful in his eyes. Dare we say larger than God.

However, are we not just the same?

We can know great victories in our lives, answered prayer, a wonderful faith-filled time of worship, seeing God working in our life and the lives of others, maybe a miraculous healing.

And then it happens just like Elijah. For us it can be something so small, but we allow a negative thought in, challenging our faith, causing us to focus on the problem in front of us, and we too can shift from being faith-filled to faithless and fearful.

'I have had enough, Lord ... Take my life' (1 Kings 19:4)

These were the words of Elijah after praying that he might die! He lay down under a bush and fell asleep. Defeated!

A human being just like us.

Elijah had allowed fear and discouragement to cloud his vision, believing that he was the only one left serving the Lord. He felt self-pity, he had just had enough.

Have you experienced this? I know I have. From being full of faith to suddenly focussing on a problem, instantly being filled with fear and dread. The shift can be tiny and happens so quickly.

You would think that God would have been fed up with Elijah. Angry even. But He wonderfully cared for him, sending an angel with food and water twice, and allowing him to sleep in between.

Later, after Elijah had rested, he had another supernatural encounter with God who spoke to him in a gentle whisper, directing him for the next step forward.

And our gracious God does the same for you and me. When we shift our focus off Him, He will get our attention somehow, showering us with His grace and mercy. He encourages us to look past the problem, to look to Him again.

I am so thankful for the way the Lord allows us to see the weakness of this great man of God. We tend to by-pass this part of his story, focussing on the great feats he accomplished in his lifetime. But God wants us to see that he was just a human being like us, he experienced the depths of despair, just as we do.

Jezebel's threat was unsuccessful. And the Lord reassured Elijah He had reserved seven thousand in Israel who had not bowed the knee to Baal.

And so, it is with us. The things we fear the most do not always happen but our thoughts can become so easily distorted that we fail to see truth.

Elijah continued to walk in faith until the end of his life and so can we.

Let's be encouraged in seeing the weakness of this man of God, a human being just like us.

When we lose focus on God let's shift our gaze back to Him. Then we can also continue to walk on in faith with Him.

"Father, so quickly we lose sight of You, and only see the giants in front of us. You are so patient with us, thank you. Please help us to keep our eyes of faith firmly fixed on You. Amen."

THE BIRD FEEDER

I love it when birds visit our garden.

Having moved into a new home we had to start over again, putting up new feeders in places we could see from indoors and waiting for the birds to build the confidence to come and feed.

Weeks went by, we waited patiently, watching in anticipation for the time when we would see the feeders attracting the variety of birds we hoped to spot near the coast.

Early spring arrived with cold weather and as I sat in the warmth of our lounge, listening to the wind howling around outside, I spotted movement. Twitching in the small bush on our patio near the feeder.

I watched, keeping my focus on the small movements in the foliage, as eventually I was rewarded by spotting the presence of a sparrow in the bush. Each twitch was bringing him a step closer until at last he flew up and just for a fragile moment tasted and knew the seed was good.

In an instant the sparrow was gone, but my patience had been rewarded. I knew he would be back.

I felt the smile of my Father. He was watching with me and used this moment of time to speak gently into my heart. He showed me I was willing to wait patiently for our first visitor to feed, knowing it would take courage for the bird to trust that all was safe.

And so it is with us. Our heavenly Father is patient in waiting for us to turn to Him, whether it is for the first time or after we have known Him sometime. He watches us flit around looking in every direction, coming a step closer, then a step back. But in His great love for us, He won't push or rush us. He wants us to make the choice to taste and see that He is good, trustworthy and kind, always. I am so thankful He was very patient with me and didn't give up. He knew one day I would put my trust in Him.

I am reminded of the verse in Luke 12:6 where Jesus says,

'Are not five sparrows sold for two pennies? And not one of them is forgotten before God.'

God cares for every creature He has made, His eye is on the sparrow, and His eye is on us too. Always waiting patiently in every circumstance for us to trust in Him.

As the weeks went by, my sparrow friend brought along a family, and our feeders were in use constantly, attracting even more birds of different varieties. It was a joy to see, and a continuous reminder of the loving care and patience of our Father who watches over us and in whom we can safely put our lives.

Taste and see that the Lord is good; blessed is the one who takes refuge in Him. (Psalm 34:8)

"Father, I'm sorry for the times I don't trust you, but I know You are safe and a refuge and good all the time. Thank you for your patience with me. Amen."

THE POWER OF WORDS

August is the month of family birthdays, ushering in lots of cakes and of course candles!

Cake has always played an important part in our family, and any form of celebration is a good excuse for trying out another new recipe.

Since the arrival of grandchildren, the tradition of singing 'Happy Birthday' and blowing out candles has taken us to another level, and re-lighting the candles and blowing them out is all part of the fun.

There is nearly always a panic to find a box of matches, involving a last-minute rush to the local shop. I found myself doing just this last week, in case my son and daughter in law didn't have any in their house. I was surprised as I stood at the self-checkout to find I needed permission to buy the matches. I was slightly irritated waiting for the shop assistant to put a code in allowing me to buy them.

But in hindsight, when I thought about it, one match has the power to burn a house down or set a forest on fire. A single match can do a lot of damage if used carelessly or put in the wrong hands.

A match on its own is just a very small piece of wood, but has immeasurable power once ignited.

I was reminded of the warnings in the Bible about a small part of the body that has the power to do a great deal of good, or cause a great deal of pain. I am referring to the tongue. The Bible in James chapter 3, under the heading of 'Taming the tongue', says that with the tongue we can:

praise our Lord and Father, and with it we can curse human beings, who have been made in God's likeness. (James 3:9)

This chapter gives us the illustration of a tongue being like a fire, it has the power to corrupt the whole body and set the whole course of one's life on fire. (James 3:6)

Vivid descriptions indeed, powerful warnings about the power of our words.

But, like the match that needs to be struck to produce a flame, the tongue needs to be activated by us to produce the words we speak that can either build up or bring us and others down.

We will all have been affected in some way by someone's cruel words spoken over us, we may remember how it made us feel. For some, it may have steered the course of their lives, affecting their value and self-worth. I know I have been on the receiving end of words that have caused me hurt, and I have learnt the need to forgive and let go of what was said. I have also spoken words I regretted, after seeing the power and effect they had on the person they were spoken to.

On the other hand, we know the power of words of kindness and encouragement spoken over our lives, words that hold the key to setting us free from burdens we carry, and situations that seem hopeless.

I love the scripture that says,

The sovereign Lord has given me a well-instructed tongue, to know the word that sustains the weary. (Isaiah 50:4)

With the help of the Holy Spirit, we can learn to tame the tongue and use it to praise God and build others up. Just like the match that can bring light into darkness, we have the power to bring light into a life, shine hope into despair, and brighten up someone's day.

"Father, forgive us when we are unwise with our words. May we always use words for good to build others up. Help us also to forgive those who have hurt us. Thank you Lord. Amen."

WAITING ON GOD

As I awake in the quiet of early morning, I can hear the sound of much needed rain after a long hot, dry spell. It ushers in a fresher, cooler air, relief not only for me but for the ground also. As I listen, I am reminded of the passage of scripture in the book of Isaiah that says,

As the rain and the snow come down from heaven, and do not return to it without watering the earth and making it bud and flourish so that it yields seed for the sower and bread for the eater, so is my word that goes out from my mouth: it will not return to me empty, but will accomplish what I desire and achieve the purpose for which I sent it. (Isaiah 55:10-11)

I wonder, are you waiting on God for something He has promised you?

Waiting, and wondering if He will ever move to accomplish what He has said to you, whispered into your heart?

You were so sure it was Him, but as the years go by, you wonder if you heard correctly? You doubt if that word was from Him, even though He confirms it repeatedly.

If this is you, be encouraged. You are in good company.

We can read about characters in the Bible who waited for promises to be fulfilled, sometimes for decades, yet they all saw God bring about what He had promised, in His time.

And there is the key – in His time! And in His way! Think of Abraham, waiting for the promised son to be born, Joseph waiting for a dream to be fulfilled, David, waiting to be King. Just three characters who waited years for God to bring about His plans for them. And I wonder, did Jesus wait patiently for thirty years until He could begin His ministry? Just a thought.

I have been waiting for the fulfilment of a promise that God gave me many years ago. I know deep-down I can trust that God will bring it about in His way and time but sometimes I doubt, sometimes I get impatient. I question God, I moan at Him.

'I can't take this anymore God,' I cry.

When I get desperate, He faithfully encourages me with a hint of what is to come, it's as if He allows me to peek through a chink in a curtain, to gain a small glimpse, just enough to give me hope, and grace to carry on for another day.

The scripture from Isaiah quoted above declares God's faithfulness to His word. There are many promises of God in the Bible, and He is always faithful to what He says He will do.

But verse ten is proceeded by verse nine that says:

'As the heavens are higher than the earth, so are my ways higher than your ways, and my thoughts than your thoughts.' (Isaiah 55:9)

Even when we think we know best and how our life should pan out, I am so thankful that our Father doesn't give in to us. His ways and thoughts are always higher, and always good, and far greater than we could ever hope for. We just don't see the bigger picture.

Don't give up if you are holding out for a promise from God. The characters in the Bible waited years for their promises but when they were fulfilled, their lives were changed, and, subsequently, nations were blessed through them. God brought about more than they could ever have asked or imagined.

Hold on, wait patiently, allow the Maker of the Universe to bring about His plans, His way, and in His time. When you see what you have been waiting for being accomplished in front of your eyes, I believe that all the pain, struggle, turmoil and unbelief will be swallowed up in an instant as you marvel at what He has done for you.

"Father, forgive us for our unbelief, forgive us when we strive to bring about our plans thinking you are too slow, or have forgotten us. Give us more of Your grace that is sufficient, keep us worshipping in the waiting, and help us to hold on, when all seems lost, when we feel abandoned. Help us to remember that You always accomplish what You seek to accomplish, and it is always good. Amen."

Beware, Angel of Light

Whilst gardening, I came across a lovely looking wildflower, or so I thought. I love wildflowers and was really pleased to find one growing in the rockery. It looked so pretty, with lovely white bushy flowers. What I didn't realise was that this was a stinging nettle growing. Our garden has a lot of nettles but I had never seen one flowering.

However pretty it looked, it was deceptive, and could produce a nasty sting!

This made me think how easily we can be fooled into thinking something is so good when in fact it is the complete opposite and will harm us if we get too close or involved, however good it looks or seems.

Isn't this just how the enemy works, tempting us in all sorts of ways to be fooled into thinking something is good when it is in truth harmful? He is the master of disguise.

It could be something obvious, like drinking too much, just one more won't harm us, or eating too much, or getting addicted to anything that will distract us from Jesus.

We don't always see what is happening but, before we know it, our eyes are off the Lord, and we are being led astray.

The Bible doesn't dwell on the enemy too much but there are warnings about the way he works, he is called the angel of light – if he showed his true colours, we would never be fooled, but he comes in disguise in many forms, any way to separate us from our Father.

One day he will be revealed for who he really is, the father of lies, the one who comes to kill steal and destroy, but until that day let us keep close to our Lord, let us test everything that seems good, but may not be, and let us not be deceived by the enemy of our souls.

The thief comes to steal and kill and destroy; I have come that they may have life, and have it to the full. (John 10:10)

And no wonder, for Satan himself masquerades as an angel of light. (2 Corinthians 11:14)

He is Still Sovereign

There is a lot of talk nowadays about climate change, and the effects of global warming. We watch as earthquakes shake our earth, hurricanes rip through countries causing so much damage, flooding occurs, fires rage across dry hot lands. This can cause uncertainty in our hearts; we can find ourselves being fearful of the changes taking place in our world and what may occur in the future.

During the summer, early one morning I sat in my garden, revelling in the quiet and stillness of another hot day to come. I was thanking God for His beautiful creation, the greenness of the trees, the blueness of the sky. Sitting there I glanced up and noticed the moon was still showing, gradually growing dim as the brightness of the day advanced.

In the peace of the morning, I was aware of my Father trying to catch my attention.

Listening to His still small voice, I was reminded of the scripture in Genesis that says:

As long as the earth endures,

seedtime and harvest,
cold and heat,
summer and winter,
day and night
will never cease. (Genesis 8:22)

Noah and his family had just come out of the ark with pairs of every living creature. They were the only ones to survive the flood. They built an altar to the Lord and sacrificed burnt offerings on it. The Lord was pleased with it and scripture says He said in His heart that He would never curse the ground because of humans again, even though the inclination of every human heart was evil from childhood and He would never destroy all living creatures as He had done in the flood. (Genesis 8:20-21)

His promise still stands for us today even though we have messed up and continue to spoil His creation with our greed and selfish ways. He is faithful in allowing the earth as we know it to endure, seasons continue, and day and night never cease. Hundreds of years later, His faithfulness to His promise still stands. He has kept true to His word.

The promise speaks of a truth that cannot be changed or shaken whatever happens around us. It is written to remind us just who is in control of this earth, even the times and seasons. We may have messed up, but God remains the King. He is still in control, He remains the same, He is never changing, and what a comfort to know this, to dwell on this and remember this always.

So great is His faithfulness to humanity

I find this incredibly comforting and reassuring. Whatever our beliefs about the climate, whatever our fears, God is sovereign over His creation and not until He ushers in a new heaven and earth will this earth as we know it cease to exist. All things will be made new, and as Christians we have this hope.

Not only is our Lord faithful to His world, but He is faithful to His people. One of my favourite scriptures and one I pray often is from Lamentations 3:21-23.

Yet, this I call to mind, and therefore I have hope, Because of the Lords great love, we are not consumed, for His compassions never fail. They are new every morning; great is Your faithfulness.'

I love this world He has created, I think it is beautiful even in its fallen state. I also love the truth that my heavenly Father is not only watching over His world but watching over me. His eye is upon me, caring for me, loving me, I am never alone and His faithfulness will carry me all the way through into eternity with Him.

"Thank you, God, that You are our refuge and strength, an ever-present help in trouble. Therefore, we will not fear though the earth give way and the mountains fall into the heart of the sea. Amen." (Psalm 46:2)

The Dustcart

The week wasn't going well. I was dealing with spiritual oppression and felt discouraged, 'got at' spiritually, and alone.

Do you ever experience weeks like this?

It seems one thing after another comes along to make you doubt God's goodness, it feels like a tripwire is there for every step you take.

The enemy, whose sole intention is to steal, kill and destroy, tries his very best to distract your gaze off Jesus and onto the chaos around you. He whispers into your mind that it's all too hard, and God doesn't seem to be there to help you. We so readily agree to these lies, and that's where I found myself this day.

Destructive and discouraging thoughts have the power to make us feel like giving up. And praying feels like walking through thick mud. We know all the scriptures we should be quoting, speaking truth out over ourselves, but our strength has gone, and we feel weak and helpless.

As the week carried on, blow after blow, I found myself driving around looking for somewhere to stop and be by myself, to de-stress, and yes, to talk to God.

I attempted to get find a space in a carpark so I could walk down to the water, but I was jammed in by a dustcart, and had to wait quite a while as the dustmen emptied all the dustbins from behind the pub. I felt anger rise within me.

Finally leaving the carpark, I turned down a road I knew led to the sea. Frustratingly I was stuck behind another dustcart, and I could see the men had a lot of rubbish bins to empty before the cart could move on.

I sat staring out of my windscreen watching them at work and had a fleeting thought at the back of my mind that the Holy Spirit had something to say to me, but I really wasn't in the mood to listen.

At last, I could move on, only to find the next road had another dustcart, and I was stuck again. By now I was really irritated but sat once more watching rubbish being emptied into the back of the truck.

Finally, I was able to drive on and found a parking space overlooking the inlet. It was high tide and the water looked beautiful, but I felt so deflated I couldn't appreciate the view.

It wasn't until later at a friend's house, sitting in her garden off-loading, that I remembered the dustcarts and found myself laughing.

My Father who loves me so much wanted to let me know that I was heavy laden and had allowed a load of rubbish to build up in my heart and mind. He was purposely allowing me to get caught behind not two but three dustcarts to give me the visual illustration of the need to offload my burdens to Him. He knew I was distracted and would need the three dustcarts collecting rubbish to get my attention!

I was reminded of the verses in Matthew 11:28-29 where Jesus says,

'Come to me, all you who are weary and burdened, and I will give you rest. Take my yoke upon you and learn from me, for I am gentle and humble in heart, and you will find rest for your souls.'

I was weary and burdened, and I so needed His rest in my heart and mind.

Once I had offloaded and asked forgiveness for allowing troubles to distract me from Him, I found the rest and peace only found in Jesus.

Are you struggling with heaviness feeling as if it's all too hard?

We can offload to our Father any time, night or day. He doesn't want us carrying heaviness and listening to the lies of the enemy. Come to Jesus who is our rest, He wants to carry our burdens, so we will find peace in Him. He has never left us, but we need to turn our eyes to Him, and off the things that burden us.

"Father, please forgive us when we carry heavy worries and burdens that weigh us down and take our focus off You. Thank you that You desire us to come to you and find rest. Thank you for Your patience with us, and that Your eye is always upon us. Amen."

Flowers in Winter

Opening the front door, there it was – a bunch of flowers laid carefully on the step – loosely wrapped in tissue paper.

My heart warmed and a smile developed slowly as I felt the blessing of the Father's love once again.

There was no note or card attached. The flowers were anonymous as always, but I knew instantly where they had come from, who had taken the trouble to listen to God and be obedient to His prompting.

You see, this was not the first time I had received this anonymous gift of flowers on my doorstep. Over the months and years that I had lived there, I lost count of the number of times flowers had been left. Sometimes fresh from the garden, spring, and summer flowers. In winter months, they were bought sprays – but always, always perfectly timed.

Winter for me is not necessarily the time of year, but it can be ushered in at any time and during those years, winter seemed to visit me often.

Hard, cold struggling days – seasons of pain and hardship, filled with the 'what ifs 'and 'supposing ifs' that battled in my mind. Seasons when I doubted God's presence, questioned His love for me, believing the lie that He had left me, and wasn't aware of my struggles.

It's in those winters of the soul, in the midst of the dark thoughts, God can feel distant, detached. I would find myself feeling unlovable, unworthy and in desperate need of assurance that all God's promises never to leave us nor forsake us were true.

And then the flowers would arrive, taking me by surprise, whisking away the doubts, and pouring Gods love into my heart once more. He had noticed, He wanted to show me how much He knew what I was going through and that nothing could separate me from His love. Nothing!

Now, years later, we have moved away into a new area, and the flowers on the doorstop have stopped. Life can still be tough at times, but I am stronger in the Lord now, and He has many ways that He continues to show me His love.

Just recently I had a birthday, I was showered with bunches of flowers, by hand and through the post. The blessings kept flowing. I recognised the hand of God, reminding me once more He knew what I needed. And I received them all from Him with thanksgiving.

I really hope my anonymous giver is thoroughly blessed for her obedience, even more so as I know her life is challenging at times. It has encouraged me to look for ways to bless others, who need to know the love of their Father, to be reassured that He has never left them and is with them always.

For I am convinced that neither death nor life, neither angels nor demons, neither the present nor the future, nor any powers, neither height nor depth, nor anything else in all creation, will be able to separate us from the love of God that is in Christ Jesus our Lord. (Romans 8:38-39)

The Beauty in Dying

It's that time of year again here in the UK. Autumn. Not my favourite season. I'm very quick to feel negative with the realisation of the onset of long dark winter days with lack of light and warmth.

As I walked today, I was enjoying the heat still left in the sun, the warmth I felt alongside a brisk chilly breeze. The sky was a deep blue and I found myself thanking God for the brightness of the morning. Boats were bobbing around in the marina waters. It felt good to be outside on such a sunny autumnal day.

My eyes were suddenly averted to a tree whose leaves were turning a brilliant red. A vivid reminder of the inevitable onset of winter. The colours were beautiful, but I felt an inner groan spoiling the day.

It was then that I felt my Father challenge me.

I felt Him say, 'There is beauty in dying'. I listened as He revealed gently the meaning to this.

I knew He was encouraging me to take note of the vibrant colours, and although the redness was the progression of death for these leaves, it was a beautiful sight and a necessary stage in the rhythm of life.

As I continued to walk, I sensed the Spirit engaging me into a deeper lesson to learn.

There is beauty in our dying. Dying to self, dying to that which would distract us away from our intimacy with the Father. There was more. He showed me that there was beauty in the death of Jesus. It ushered in new life and forgiveness for those who would choose Him as Saviour. There is beauty too in our physical death, as we pass into all that awaits us in the fullness of eternity.

Later, walking back to the car, I was still dwelling on these insights. I felt the Spirit say, 'Sometimes things have to die to bring about the new'. I thought about this for a while.

I believe He was challenging me is to trust and be willing to die to old ways - my plans, my agendas - and in doing so revival would come in and through me, allowing new things to grow and flourish in my life, touching others as an overflow of His work in my life.

I believe this is a challenge to all who know and love the Lord.

Are we willing to surrender ourselves to Him, to die to ourselves and allow His Spirit to renew us within?

I believe our Father sees this as a beautiful act of worship.

Just as the autumnal leaves turning a glorious red in colour as they die, we too will reveal more of His beauty through our dying to self.

But one day is coming when all will be revived to its former glory as He ushers in the new heaven and earth and finally death will be no more.

A Taste of Glory

Do you think often about heaven?

I wonder, have you ever imagined what it will be like, to finally be there?

On a good day, you may not think much about it. You may see God in His creation, and think how wonderful heaven is going to be, you may try to imagine what it will be like to see God face to face.

It's good to dwell on such things, catching a glimpse of what is to come, to live with our heavenly Father forever in a glorious new heaven and earth.

We may find eternity difficult to comprehend because we live in time, and in moments of time, and the fullness of eternity is outside of time. God has always been, there was no beginning to God, nor is there any end to God. And God lives outside of time and sees the beginning, middle and end of our earthly life. If you have given your life to Christ, He already sees you in eternity with Him.

And God raised us up with Christ and seated us with Him in the heavenly realms in Christ Jesus (Ephesians 2:6)

Eternal life starts at birth, everybody is heading towards an eternity with or without God.

On a bad day, when you are struggling, it's hard to imagine what it will be like to be in a place where there will be no more suffering, tears or pain. Maybe you have been so desperate that you wanted Jesus to take you now? Tragically, many people who don't know God think that to die is an escape from this life, without even knowing what is beyond the grave. They do not have the hope that is found only in Christ.

One morning I was worshipping God as I drove into work. I was having a bad start to the day. I felt anxious and alone as I sat stuck in a traffic jam. But as I sang along with the worship song that was playing, for just for a moment I was lifted out of the darkness encircling me, and into an experience that I can only describe as heavenly. The song had reached a crescendo and people were singing in the Spirit, the volume was high, and as I joined in, I felt myself surrounded by a great volume of worshippers. I experienced just a sense of what it may feel like to be whole and healthy and completely free. The fullness of joy was overwhelming. The sound of worshippers was incredible. Just for a minute I tasted something of what is to come. And I am so thankful to God for that one moment in time. I believe my Father allowed me to experience a taste of glory.

As time has gone by, I have lost the feeling I experienced on that journey to work, but I will always remember how wonderful it was, truly heavenly!

Maybe as your read this you are in a time of suffering, and you long for it to end, you long to escape. It could be a broken marriage, relationship, illness, physical handicap, depression, heartache of some kind, loss, grief, pain, or unemployment.

Do you believe your pain can have a purpose if given to God? Your problems, struggles, and heartaches can lead you towards one end - the glory of God. It seems hard to believe when you are in the midst of it, but God will turn it around for His glory and He promises to be with you in it.

When you long to escape, God is with you, hold tight, nothing is wasted with Him.

Life is full of moments. Some seem good, some bad, feeling like they may last for ever, but in truth they are just a moment in time.

We are heading towards a glorious day, when we will finally arrive at our heavenly home. There I believe we will look back and see our whole life in the light of eternity, and then, finally we will understand.

'Call on me in the day of trouble; I will deliver you, and you will honour me' (Psalm 50:15)

"Father, thank you we have this hope, Eternal life with You. We see so dimly now, but one day we will experience the fullness of heaven, and finally we will see You face to face. Please help us to remember this as we journey through this world, especially through the difficult times. In Jesus name, Amen."

EPILOGUE

Walking Home

It was a very cold day for walking. Mid-winter, nearing the shortest day of the year, and the light was fading fast. I was tempted to turn back but encouraged myself on towards the water.

No one was about, the air was so still, and it was icy cold as I made my way along the footpath across the fields. Hands in pockets, hat pulled down, I carried on, determined to at least catch a glimpse of the sea.

As I reached the bank leading up to the water, I stood looking over the inlet, the tide was up and as always it was a beautiful sight. I rested for a few minutes, soaking up the peace and stillness, aware that My Father was with me, and enjoying my company. I smiled as I soaked up the atmosphere. However, I didn't dwell long because it was bitterly cold, and I could feel the iciness invading me through my thick clothing.

On turning around I was now on my return journey, heading back towards warmth, light and a hot cup of tea. I started to walk faster, I wanted to get home before dark.

It was then that I felt the familiar nudge that I had come to recognise as my heavenly Father.

I felt Him tell me that my whole life I had been heading home. Every day, every hour, every second, every moment in time, I had been walking a journey towards my Eternal home, every step bringing me nearer to heaven.

He was beckoning me to look forward to a time when there would be no more struggling or pain. My temporary walk through this life would one day usher me into life in eternity with Him, finally whole, and perfectly fulfilled in Him.

As I continued my journey home, I pondered on these insights, until finally I was welcomed by a warm home and hot drink, glowing from the invigorating walk.

Over the following days, I continued to dwell on what my Father had shared with me. I was so thankful for the encouragement.

Even though I love this world He has created, and I am aware of the life He lives in me, I always carry the hope of what is to come, at the end of my life's journey.

I pray these devotionals have reached your heart, and that you have heard the whisper of your heavenly Father speaking love and encouragement to you.

He is also beckoning you to look forward to a time when there will be no more struggling or pain, our temporary walk through this life will be over, and we will live in eternity with Him.

I'll see you there sometime...... what a day that will be. I can't wait, can you?